e World's Greatest Sports Stars The World's Greatest Sports Stars
e World's Greatest Sports Stars The World's Greatest Sports Stars
e World's Greatest Spor The World's Greatest Sports Stars

Sports Illustrated KIDS

The World's Greatest
Basketball Players

by Matt Doeden

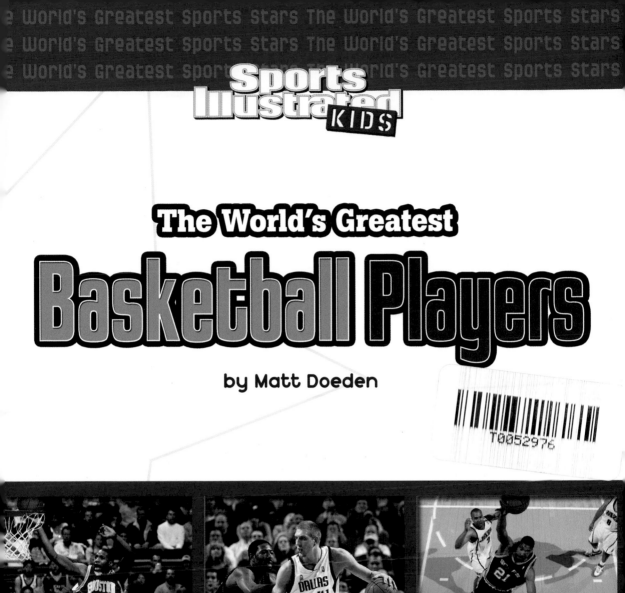

T0052976

CAPSTONE PRESS
a capstone imprint

Sports Illustrated KIDS The World's Greatest Sports Stars is published by Capstone Press, 1710 Roe Crest Drive, North Mankato, Minnesota 56003. www.capstonepub.com

Library of Congress Cataloging-in-Publication Data
Doeden, Matt.
   The world's greatest basketball players / by Matt Doeden.
   p. cm. — (Sports Illustrated KIDS. the world's greatest sports stars)
   Includes bibliographical references and index.
   Summary: "Describes the achievements and career statistics of basketball's greatest stars" — Provided by publisher.
   ISBN 978-1-4296-3923-1 (library binding)
   ISBN 978-1-4296-4869-1 (paperback)
   ISBN 978-1-4765-0192-5 (e-book)
   1. Basketball players — Biography — Juvenile literature. 2. Basketball players — Rating of — Juvenile literature. I. Title. II. Series.
GV884.A1D64 2010
796.323092'2 — dc22
[B]   2009028535

Editorial Credits
Aaron Sautter, editor; Tracy Davies, designer; Eric Gohl, media researcher; Laura Manthe, production specialist

Photo Credits
Shutterstock/Ksash, backgrounds
Sports Illustrated/Bill Frakes, 1 (left), 18; Bob Rosato, 1 (center), 11, 12, 28; Damian Strohmeyer, 6, 8, 17; John Biever, 5 (both), 25; John W. McDonough, cover, 1 (right), 4 (left), 15, 21, 22, 26; Manny Millan, 4–5 (background), 4 (right), 30–31 (background)

Statistics in this book are current through the 2011–12 NBA season.

Printed and bound in China. PO5070

Table of Contents

Game On!. 4

Kobe Bryant. 6

Kevin Garnett 8

Dirk Nowitzki 11

Tim Duncan. 12

Chris Paul 15

LeBron James 17

Dwight Howard. 18

Kevin Durant. 21

Tracy McGrady 22

Paul Pierce. 25

Brandon Roy 26

Dwyane Wade. 28

Glossary 30

Read More 31

Internet Sites 31

Index. 32

Game On!

Swish! Kobe Bryant sinks a long three-pointer. Thud! Tim Duncan blocks a shot before the ball goes in the net. Basketball is packed with action. Fans across the country love watching monster dunks and long-range bombs. The biggest stars of the National Basketball Association (NBA) bring loads of excitement to the court.

slam **dunks**   big-time **blocks**

amazing **shots**   intense **action**

Kobe Bryant

Kobe Bryant thrives in the clutch. The Los Angeles Lakers guard is at his best when the game is on the line. He can shoot from the outside or drive into the lane and score inside. Bryant is a great defender too. He's been selected to the NBA's All-Defensive First Team seven times. Bryant was the 2007–2008 NBA Most Valuable Player (MVP). He is also a five-time NBA champion.

Regular Season Stats

Year	Team	Games	PPG	RPG	APG	SPG
1996–1997	LAL	71	7.6	1.9	1.3	0.7
1997–1998	LAL	79	15.4	3.1	2.5	0.9
1998–1999	LAL	50	19.9	5.3	3.8	1.4
1999–2000	LAL	66	22.5	6.3	4.9	1.6
2000–2001	LAL	68	28.5	5.9	5.0	1.7
2001–2002	LAL	80	25.2	5.5	5.5	1.5
2002–2003	LAL	82	30.0	6.9	5.9	2.2
2003–2004	LAL	65	24.0	5.5	5.1	1.7
2004–2005	LAL	66	27.6	5.9	6.0	1.3
2005–2006	LAL	80	35.4	5.3	4.5	1.8
2006–2007	LAL	77	31.6	5.7	5.4	1.4
2007–2008	LAL	82	28.3	6.3	5.4	1.8
2008–2009	LAL	82	26.8	5.2	4.9	1.5
2009–2010	LAL	73	27.0	5.4	5.0	1.5
2010–2011	LAL	82	25.3	5.1	4.7	1.2
2011–2012	LAL	58	27.9	5.4	4.6	1.2
CAREER		**1,161**	**25.4**	**5.3**	**4.7**	**1.5**

(PPG = points per game; RPG = rebounds per game;
APG = assists per game; SPG = steals per game)

achievements

All-Star selection: 1998, 2000, 2001, 2002, 2003, 2004,
      2005, 2006, 2007, 2008, 2009, 2010, 2011, 2012
All-Star Game MVP: 2002, 2007, 2009
NBA MVP: 2007–2008
NBA Finals MVP: 2009, 2011
NBA All-Defensive First Team: 2000, 2003, 2004, 2006,
      2007, 2008, 2009, 2010, 2011
Averaged career-high 35.4 points per game in 2005–06

clutch: a crucial moment in a game when an important play must be made

fact Bryant's father is Joe "Jellybean" Bryant. He played for the Philadelphia 76ers, San Diego Clippers, and Houston Rockets.

Kevin Garnett

Kevin Garnett can do almost anything on a basketball court. He can grab **rebounds**. He can score inside. And he has a soft shooting touch. He can also pass like a guard or defend almost any player. In 2004 "The Big Ticket" won the league MVP award with the Minnesota Timberwolves. In 2008 he led the Boston Celtics to an NBA championship.

Regular Season Stats

Year	Team	Games	PPG	RPG	APG	BPG
1995–1996	MIN	80	10.4	6.3	1.8	1.6
1996–1997	MIN	77	17.0	8.0	3.1	2.1
1997–1998	MIN	82	18.5	9.6	4.2	1.8
1998–1999	MIN	47	20.8	10.4	4.3	1.8
1999–2000	MIN	81	22.9	11.8	5.0	1.6
2000–2001	MIN	81	22.0	11.4	5.0	1.8
2001–2002	MIN	81	21.2	12.1	5.2	1.6
2002–2003	MIN	82	23.0	13.4	6.0	1.6
2003–2004	MIN	82	24.2	13.9	5.0	2.2
2004–2005	MIN	82	22.2	13.5	5.7	1.4
2005–2006	MIN	76	21.8	12.7	4.1	1.4
2006–2007	MIN	76	22.4	12.8	4.1	1.7
2007–2008	BOS	71	18.8	9.2	3.4	1.3
2008–2009	BOS	57	15.8	8.5	2.5	1.2
2009–2010	BOS	69	14.3	7.3	2.7	0.8
2010–2011	BOS	71	14.9	8.9	2.4	0.8
2011–2012	BOS	60	15.8	8.2	2.9	1.0
CAREER		**1,255**	**19.3**	**10.6**	**4.0**	**1.5**

(PPG = points per game; RPG = rebounds per game;
APG = assists per game; BPG= blocks per game)

rebound: to gain possession of the ball after someone attempts a shot at the basket

achievements

All-Star selection: 1997, 1998, 2000, 2001, 2002, 2003, 2004, 2005, 2006, 2007, 2008, 2009, 2010, 2011
All-Star Game MVP: 2003
NBA MVP: 2004
NBA Defensive Player of the Year: 2008
NBA champion: 2008

fact | Garnett averaged at least 20 points, 10 rebounds, and five assists per game for a record six straight seasons.

9

Name: Dirk Nowitzki
Born: June 19, 1978, in Wurzburg, Germany
Height: 7 feet
Weight: 245 pounds
Position: Forward

Regular Season Stats

Year	Team	Games	PPG	RPG	APG	SPG
1998–1999	DAL	47	8.2	3.4	1.0	0.6
1999–2000	DAL	82	17.5	6.5	2.5	0.8
2000–2001	DAL	82	21.8	9.2	2.1	1.0
2001–2002	DAL	76	23.4	9.9	2.4	1.1
2002–2003	DAL	80	25.1	9.9	3.0	1.4
2003–2004	DAL	77	21.8	8.7	2.7	1.2
2004–2005	DAL	78	26.1	9.7	3.1	1.2
2005–2006	DAL	81	26.6	9.0	2.8	0.7
2006–2007	DAL	78	24.6	8.8	3.4	0.7
2007–2008	DAL	77	23.6	8.6	3.5	0.7
2008–2009	DAL	81	25.9	8.0	2.4	0.8
2009–2010	DAL	81	25.0	7.3	2.7	0.9
2010–2011	DAL	73	23.0	7.4	2.6	0.5
2011–2012	DAL	62	21.6	7.3	2.2	0.7
CAREER		**1,055**	**22.9**	**8.2**	**2.6**	**0.9**

(PPG= points per game; RPG = rebounds per game;
APG = assists per game; SPG = steals per game)

achievements

All-Star selection: 2003, 2004, 2005, 2006,
    2007, 2008, 2009, 2010, 2011, 2012
NBA MVP: 2007
All-NBA First Team: 2005, 2006, 2007, 2009
NBA Three-Point Shootout winner: 2006
NBA Finals MVP: 2011

fact

Nowitzki had the honor of carrying
Germany's flag in the Opening Ceremonies
of the 2008 Olympic Games.

Dirk Nowitzki

Big men like Dirk Nowitzki don't usually have the skills of a shooting guard. But he handles and passes the ball with ease. Nowitzki is also a great inside scorer and rebounder for the Dallas Mavericks. His great all-around play earned Nowitzki NBA MVP honors for the 2006–2007 season. He led the Mavericks to an NBA championship in 2011.

Tim Duncan

Tim Duncan isn't flashy, but he's a winner. The San Antonio Spurs forward rarely shows emotion on the court. But he's a real force in the **paint**. Duncan is a great rebounder and inside scorer. He's one of the league's best defenders too. Duncan's skills have helped him win two MVP awards and four NBA championships.

Name: Timothy Theodore Duncan
Born: April 25, 1976, in St. Croix, U.S. Virgin Islands
College: Wake Forest University
Height: 6 feet 11 inches   Weight: 248 pounds
Position: Forward / Center

Regular Season Stats

Year	Team	Games	PPG	RPG	APG	BPG
1997–1998	SAS	82	21.1	11.9	2.7	2.5
1998–1999	SAS	50	21.7	11.4	2.4	2.5
1999–2000	SAS	74	23.2	12.4	3.2	2.2
2000–2001	SAS	82	22.2	12.2	3.0	2.3
2001–2002	SAS	82	25.5	12.7	3.7	2.5
2002–2003	SAS	81	23.3	12.9	3.9	2.9
2003–2004	SAS	69	22.3	12.4	3.1	2.7
2004–2005	SAS	66	20.3	11.1	2.7	2.6
2005–2006	SAS	80	18.6	11.0	3.2	2.0
2006–2007	SAS	80	20.0	10.6	3.4	2.4
2007–2008	SAS	78	19.3	11.3	2.8	1.9
2008–2009	SAS	75	19.3	10.7	3.5	1.7
2009–2010	SAS	78	17.9	10.1	3.2	1.5
2010–2011	SAS	76	13.4	8.9	2.7	1.9
2011–2012	SAS	58	15.4	9.0	2.3	1.5
CAREER		**1,1111**	**20.3**	**11.3**	**3.1**	**2.2**

achievements

All-Star selection: 1998, 2000, 2001, 2002, 2003,
    2004, 2005, 2006, 2007, 2008, 2009, 2010, 2011
NBA MVP: 2002, 2003
Rookie of the Year: 1998
NBA Finals MVP: 1999, 2003, 2005
NBA champion: 1999, 2003, 2005, 2007

paint: the painted area directly below and in front of the basket

fact

Duncan grew up wanting to be a swimmer.
He switched to basketball after a hurricane
destroyed the only large pool near his home.

Name: Christopher Emmanuel Paul
Born: May 6, 1985, in Winston-Salem,
    North Carolina
College: Wake Forest University
Height: 6 feet   Weight: 175 pounds
Position: Guard

Regular Season Stats

Year	Team	Games	PPG	RPG	APG	SPG
2005–2006	NOR	78	16.1	5.1	7.8	2.2
2006–2007	NOR	64	17.3	4.4	8.9	1.8
2007–2008	NOR	80	21.1	4.0	11.6	2.7
2008–2009	NOR	78	22.8	5.5	11.0	2.8
2009–2010	NOR	45	18.7	4.2	10.7	2.1
2010–2011	NOR	80	15.9	4.1	9.8	2.4
2011–2012	LAC	60	19.8	3.6	9.1	2.5
CAREER		**485**	**18.8**	**4.5**	**9.8**	**2.4**

(PPG = points per game; RPG = rebounds per game;
APG = assists per game; SPG = steals per game)

achievements

All-Star selection: 2008, 2009, 2010, 2011, 2012
Rookie of the Year Award: 2006
NBA assists leader: 2008, 2009
NBA steals leader: 2006, 2008, 2009, 2011, 2012
All-NBA First Team: 2008, 2009, 2012

fact

Paul set an NBA record by making at
least one steal in 108 straight games.

Chris Paul

Nobody drives into the paint or passes like the Los Angeles Clippers' Chris Paul. If a shot is open, he'll take it. If not, he'll pass the ball to an open teammate. Paul's great passing and quick hands makes him one of the league's best point guards. He has led the NBA in steals five seasons and in assists two seasons.

Name: LeBron Raymone James
Born: December 30, 1984, in Akron, Ohio
Height: 6 feet, 8 inches
Weight: 240 pounds
Position: Forward

Regular Season Stats

Year	Team	Games	PPG	RPG	APG	SPG
2003–2004	CLE	79	20.9	5.5	5.9	1.6
2004–2005	CLE	80	27.2	7.4	7.2	2.2
2005–2006	CLE	79	31.4	7.0	6.6	1.6
2006–2007	CLE	78	27.3	6.7	6.0	1.6
2007–2008	CLE	75	30.0	7.9	7.2	1.8
2008–2009	CLE	81	28.4	7.6	7.2	1.7
2009–2010	CLE	76	29.7	7.3	8.6	1.6
2010–2011	MIA	79	26.7	7.5	7.0	1.6
2011–2012	MIA	62	27.1	7.9	6.2	1.9
CAREER		**689**	**27.6**	**7.2**	**6.9**	**1.7**

(PPG = points per game; RPG = rebounds per game;
APG = assists per game; SPG = steals per game)

achievements

All-Star selection: 2005, 2006, 2007,
        2008, 2009, 2010, 2011, 2012
All-Star Game MVP: 2006, 2008
NBA MVP: 2009, 2010, 2012
Rookie of the Year Award: 2004
All-NBA First Team: 2006, 2008, 2009,
        2010, 2011, 2012
NBA scoring champion: 2008

fact In 2008 James helped the U.S. team win the gold medal in the Olympics.

LeBron James

Nobody's going to stop LeBron James when he wants to score. James has a rare combination of speed and strength. He's almost impossible to guard. James was a huge star even before he was a pro. In 2003 he went straight from high school to the Cleveland Cavaliers. James led the Heat to an NBA title in 2012, earning an MVP and a Finals MVP.

Dwight Howard

Dwight Howard is a beast in the paint. Nobody works harder to block the ball and grab rebounds. The Orlando Magic made him the top pick of the 2004 NBA **Draft**. He is one of the NBA's best rebounders. Howard knows how to put up points too. Put it all together and he's one of the best "big men" in the NBA.

Name: Dwight David Howard
Born: December 8, 1985, in Atlanta, Georgia
Height: 6 feet 11 inches
Weight: 240 pounds
Position: Center

Regular Season Stats

Year	Team	Games	PPG	RPG	APG	BPG
2004–2005	ORL	82	12.0	10.0	0.9	1.7
2005–2006	ORL	82	15.8	12.5	1.5	1.4
2006–2007	ORL	82	17.6	12.3	1.9	1.9
2007–2008	ORL	82	20.7	14.2	1.3	2.1
2008–2009	ORL	79	20.6	13.8	1.4	2.9
2009–2010	ORL	82	18.3	13.2	1.8	2.8
2010–2011	ORL	78	22.9	14.1	1.4	2.4
2011–2012	ORL	54	20.6	14.5	1.9	2.1
CAREER		**621**	**18.4**	**13.0**	**1.5**	**2.2**

(PPG = points per game; RPG = rebounds per game;
APG = assists per game; BPG = blocks per game)

achievements

All-Star selection: 2007, 2008, 2009, 2010,
   2011, 2012
All-NBA First Team: 2008, 2009, 2010, 2011, 2012
Led NBA in total rebounds: 2006, 2007,
   2008, 2009, 2010, 2012
Youngest player in NBA history to reach
   5,000 career rebounds
Number-one overall pick of 2004 NBA Draft

draft: an event when an athlete is chosen to join a professional sports team

fact

Howard won the 2008 NBA All-Star Slam Dunk Contest. In one of his dunks, he wore a Superman cape. He took off from beyond the free-throw line to make a huge slam dunk.

Name: Kevin Wayne Durant
Born: September 29, 1988, in Washington, D.C.
Height: 6 feet 9 inches
Weight: 215 pounds
Position: Forward

Regular Season Stats

Year	Team	Games	PPG	RPG	APG	SPG
2007–2008	SEA	80	20.3	4.4	2.4	1.0
2008–2009	OKC	74	25.3	6.5	2.8	1.3
2009–2010	OKC	82	30.1	7.6	2.8	1.4
2010–2011	OKC	78	27.7	6.8	2.7	1.1
2011–2012	OKC	66	28.0	8.0	3.5	1.3
CAREER		**380**	**26.3**	**6.6**	**2.8**	**1.2**

(PPG = points per game; RPG = rebounds per game
APG = assists per game; SPG = steals per game)

achievements

Second overall pick of the 2007 NBA Draft
Rookie of the Year: 2008
All-Star selection: 2010, 2011, 2012
NBA scoring leader: 2010, 2011, 2012
NBA free throw leader: 2010, 2011, 2012
All-NBA First Team: 2010, 2011, 2012

fact | Behind Kevin Durant and Russell Westbrook, the Thunder stormed to the 2012 NBA Finals before losing to the Miami Heat.

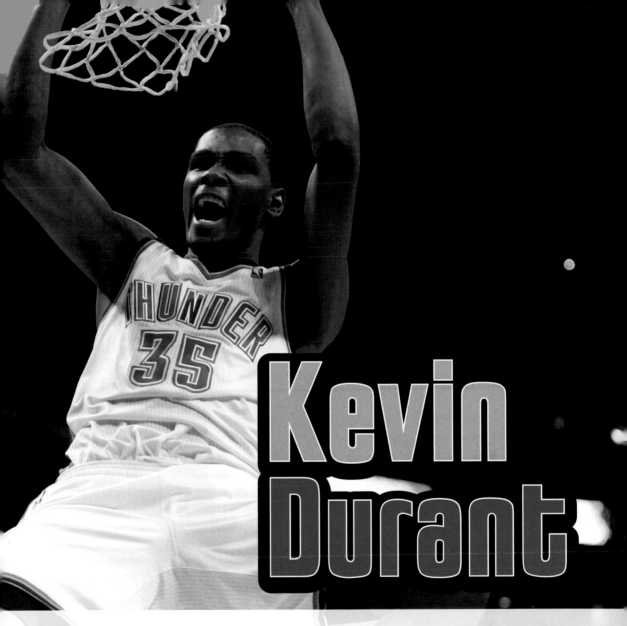

Kevin Durant

Kevin Durant's college success immediately carried over into the NBA. A star from the University of Texas, Durant averaged 20.3 points with the SuperSonics in his first NBA season. He earned the 2008 Rookie of the Year award, and he's only become better with the Oklahoma City Thunder. He has led the league in scoring three straight years.

Tracy McGrady

Tracy McGrady can score from almost anywhere on the court. He can slash toward the hoop for a **layup**. Or he can step back and launch a long three-pointer. McGrady was the NBA's scoring champ twice while with the Orlando Magic. Injuries have slowed his career, but when he's on the court, he can still be a solid all-around player.

Regular Season Stats

Year	Team	Games	PPG	RPG	APG	SPG
1997–1998	TOR	64	7.0	4.2	1.5	0.8
1998–1999	TOR	49	9.3	5.7	2.3	1.1
1999–2000	TOR	79	15.4	6.3	3.3	1.1
2000–2001	ORL	77	26.8	7.5	4.6	1.5
2001–2002	ORL	76	25.6	7.9	5.3	1.6
2002–2003	ORL	75	32.1	6.5	5.5	1.7
2003–2004	ORL	67	28.0	6.0	5.5	1.4
2004–2005	HOU	78	25.7	6.2	5.7	1.7
2005–2006	HOU	47	24.4	6.5	4.8	1.3
2006–2007	HOU	71	24.6	5.3	6.5	1.3
2007–2008	HOU	66	21.6	5.1	5.9	1.0
2008–2009	HOU	35	15.6	4.4	5.0	1.2
2009–2010	NYK	24	8.2	3.1	3.3	0.5
2010–2011	DET	72	8.0	3.5	3.5	0.9
2011–2012	ATL	52	5.3	3.0	2.1	0.3
CAREER		**938**	**19.6**	**5.6**	**4.4**	**1.2**

(PPG = points per game; RPG = rebounds per game;
APG = assists per game; SPG = steals per game)

achievements

All-Star selection: 2001, 2002, 2003, 2004,
    2005, 2006, 2007
NBA Most Improved Player Award: 2001
All-NBA First Team: 2002, 2003
NBA scoring champion: 2002, 2003
Made NBA record 8 three-pointers in one half
    on January 26, 2004

layup: a shot where the ball is gently played off the backboard and into the basket

fact

McGrady and the Orlando Magic's Vince Carter are third cousins. They both played for the Toronto Raptors in the late 1990s.

Name: Paul Anthony Pierce
Born: October 13, 1977, in Oakland, California
College: University of Kansas
Height: 6 feet 7 inches   **Weight:** 235 pounds
Position: Forward

Regular Season Stats

Year	Team	Games	PPG	RPG	APG	SPG
1998–1999	BOS	48	16.5	6.4	2.4	1.7
1999–2000	BOS	73	19.5	5.4	3.0	2.1
2000–2001	BOS	82	25.3	6.4	3.1	1.7
2001–2002	BOS	82	26.1	6.9	3.2	1.9
2002–2003	BOS	79	25.9	7.3	4.4	1.8
2003–2004	BOS	80	23.0	6.5	5.1	1.6
2004–2005	BOS	82	21.6	6.6	4.2	1.6
2005–2006	BOS	79	26.8	6.7	4.7	1.4
2006–2007	BOS	47	25.0	5.9	4.1	1.0
2007–2008	BOS	80	19.6	5.1	4.5	1.3
2008–2009	BOS	81	20.5	5.6	3.6	1.0
2009–2010	BOS	71	18.3	4.4	3.1	1.2
2010–2011	BOS	80	18.9	5.4	3.3	1.0
2011–2012	BOS	61	19.4	5.2	4.5	1.1
CAREER		**1,025**	**22.0**	**6.0**	**3.8**	**1.5**

(PPG = points per game; RPG = rebounds per game;
APG = assists per game; SPG = steals per game)

achievements

All-Star selection: 2002, 2003, 2004, 2005,
     2006, 2008, 2009, 2010, 2011, 2012
NBA Finals MVP: 2008
NBA champion: 2008
NBA All-Rookie First Team: 1999
NCAA First-Team All-America: 1998

fact Pierce's nickname is "The Truth." It was
given to him by center Shaquille O'Neal.

Paul Pierce

In Game 1 of the 2008 NBA Finals, Boston's Paul Pierce injured his knee. But he shrugged off the pain and returned to the court. He led the Celtics to a victory. The team went on to win the NBA title. Pierce's sweet shooting and tough play made him the NBA Finals MVP that season.

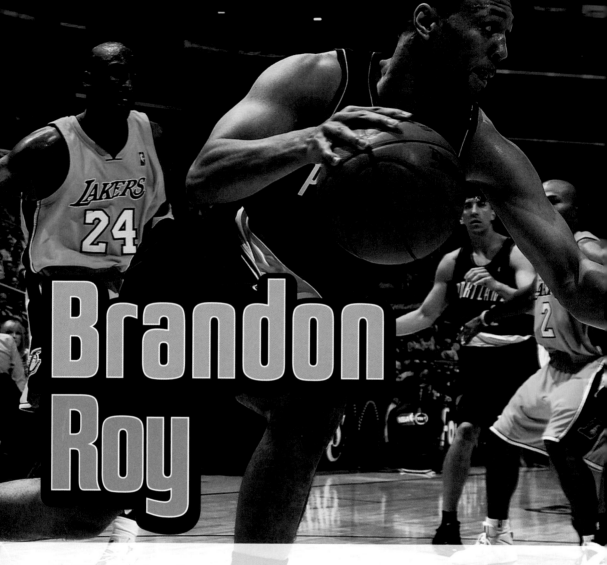

Brandon Roy

Brandon Roy quickly made his mark in the NBA. In 2006 he scored 20 points in his first game with the Portland Trail Blazers. Then he scored 19 in his second game. Roy's accurate shooting, passing ability, and good defense made him the **Rookie** of the Year in 2007. By his second year, he was already an All-Star. Roy didn't play in 2011 because of injuries, but he signed with the Minnesota Timberwolves in 2012.

Name: Brandon Dawayne Roy
Born: July 23, 1984, in Seattle, Washington
College: University of Washington
Height: 6 feet 6 inches
Weight: 211 pounds
Position: Guard

Regular Season stats

Year	Team	Games	PPG	RPG	APG	SPG
2006–2007	POR	57	16.8	4.4	4.0	1.2
2007–2008	POR	74	19.1	4.7	5.8	1.1
2008–2009	POR	78	22.6	4.7	5.1	1.1
2009–2010	POR	65	21.5	4.4	4.7	0.9
2010–2011	POR	47	12.2	2.6	2.7	0.8
CAREER		**321**	**19.0**	**4.3**	**4.7**	**1.0**

(PPG = points per game; RPG = rebounds per game;
APG = assists per game; SPG = steals per game)

rookie: a first-year player

achievements

All-Star selection: 2008, 2009, 2010
Rookie of the Year Award: 2007
Pacific Ten Conference Player of the Year: 2006
NCAA All-American: 2006
Scored game-high 18 points at 2008 All-Star Game

fact | On January 24, 2009, Roy had 10 steals in one game. His effort set a Portland record.

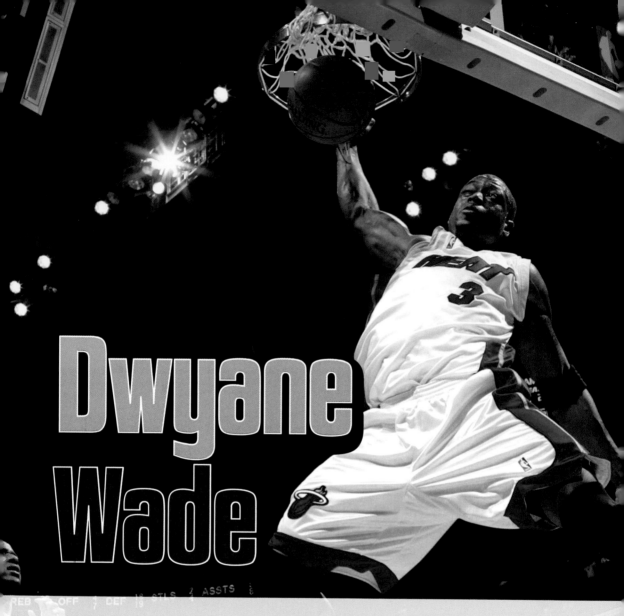

Dwyane Wade

One of Dwyane Wade's nicknames is "Flash." It's no secret why. Wade is lightning-quick with the basketball. He can beat almost any defender off the **dribble**. He can also slash to the basket or pass to an open teammate. In the 2006 NBA Finals, Wade averaged 34.7 points per game while leading the Miami Heat to the championship. He became an NBA champion again in 2012.

Name: Dwyane Tyrone Wade
Born: January 17, 1982, in Chicago, Illinois
College: Marquette University
Height: 6 feet 4 inches
Weight: 216 pounds
Position: Guard

Regular Season Stats

Year	Team	Games	PPG	RPG	APG	SPG
2003–2004	MIA	61	16.2	4.0	4.5	1.4
2004–2005	MIA	77	24.1	5.2	6.8	1.6
2005–2006	MIA	75	27.2	5.7	6.7	1.9
2006–2007	MIA	51	27.4	4.7	7.5	2.1
2007–2008	MIA	51	24.6	4.2	6.9	1.7
2008–2009	MIA	79	30.2	5.0	7.5	2.2
2009–2010	MIA	77	26.6	4.8	6.5	1.8
2010–2011	MIA	76	25.5	6.4	4.6	1.5
2011–2012	MIA	49	22.1	4.8	4.6	1.7
CAREER		**596**	**25.2**	**5.1**	**6.2**	**1.8**

(PPG = points per game; RPG = rebounds per game;
APG = assists per game; SPG = steals per game)

achievements

All-Star selection: 2005, 2006, 2007, 2008, 2009
2010, 2011, 2012
NBA All-Star Game MVP: 2010
NBA champion: 2006, 2012
NBA Finals MVP: 2006
All-NBA First Team: 2005, 2006
Member of U.S. Olympic gold medal team: 2008

dribble: to bounce the ball off the floor

fact

In 2003 Wade led the Marquette Golden Eagles to the NCAA's Final Four. He was named a First-Team All-America for his performance.

Index

Boston Celtics, 8, 25
Bryant, Kobe, 4, 6–7

Carter, Vince, 23
Cleveland Cavaliers, 17

Dallas Mavericks, 11
Duncan, Tim, 4, 12–13
Durant, Kevin, 20–21

Garnett, Kevin, 8–9

Houston Rockets, 7, 21, 22
Howard, Dwight, 18–19

James, LeBron, 16–17

Los Angeles Lakers, 6

McGrady, Tracy, 22–23
Miami Heat, 28
Minnesota Timberwolves, 8

National Basketball
    Association (NBA), 4
NBA championships, 6, 8, 12,
    25, 28
NBA Draft, 18, 21

New Orleans Hornets, 15
nicknames, 8, 24, 28
Nowitzki, Dirk, 10–11

Olympic Games, 10, 16
Orlando Magic, 18, 22, 23

Paul, Chris, 14–15
Pierce, Paul, 24–25
Portland Trail Blazers, 26

records, 9, 14, 27
Roy, Brandon, 26–27

San Antonio Spurs, 12

Wade, Dwyane, 28–29